I0776254

Putin's Orders For Trump

Do they exist, and is Trump complying?

William Dunkerley

Copyright © 2017 by William Dunkerley

ALL RIGHTS RESERVED

No part of this publication may be reproduced in any way without the prior express written consent of the copyright owner.

Published by
Omnicom Press
New Britain, CT, USA
Publishers since 1981

www.OmnicomPress.com

ISBN-13: 978-1979534529
ISBN-10: 1979534527
Printed in the United States of America

Putin's Orders For Trump *is part of the "Russia: Straight Talk on Hushed Issues" monograph series. It is dedicated to the concept of a safe, sustaining, and positive relationship between the United States and the Russian Federation.*

A list of other monographs in this series can be found at:

www.OmnicomPress.com/monographs

CONTENTS

Chapter 1
PUTIN'S PUPPET

During 2016, allegations flew left and right about how Putin was pulling Trump's strings. It was a major issue in the presidential campaign.

Check out these headlines:

"Does Vladimir Putin really own Donald Trump? It's more likely than you think" --*Salon*

"How Putin Controls Trump" --*Daily Kos*

"Why does Trump go googly-eyed for Putin?" --*Washington Post*

"Donald Trump and the Puppeteer" --*New York Times*

More headlines are cited in Chapter 2.

I filed several reports in 2016 examining a few aspects of the "Putin's puppet" allegation. They are presented in the following chapters to serve as background for the present day situation. Note that since the reports were written as standalone pieces, you may encounter some duplication.

Chapter 2
PUTIN-TRUMP OUTED

Filed: July 29, 2016

On Monday, July 18, 2016, a startling *Forbes* magazine article reported that Donald Trump is following orders from Vladimir Putin.

But that's just the start of this drama.

The following Friday, evidence surfaced that the Democratic Party primaries had been rigged so Hillary Clinton could prevail over Bernie Sanders. That same day a barrage of news items began trumpeting the alleged Trump-Putin alliance.

Headlines included:

"Donald Trump: the Siberian Candidate" --*New*

York Times

"New questions surround Putin's interest in Trump's election" --MSNBC

"GOP Rocked by Clinton Truth Bomb That Russia Is Helping Trump" --*PoliticusUSA*

And then by Sunday, July 24, a confluence emerged between these two seemingly disparate stories, i.e. the Trump-Putin allegation and the rigged primary scandal.

This is where the hand of candidate Hillary Clinton became quite visible.

What Did Hillary Do?

Clinton's campaign let loose a deviously clever strategy that drew the disparate stories together.

It cast Clinton as a victim of foul play instead of as a perpetrator of election rigging.

The short version of the scenario goes like this:

Trump and Putin are in cahoots. To help Trump, Putin has the Democratic Party's servers hacked. Putin uncovers the plot to unfairly defeat Sanders. The plot is revealed by Wikileaks.

Since most Americans look upon Putin as a loathsome and dangerous foreign leader, it's easy for many to sympathize with Hillary for falling victim to Putin.

No Facts

Mind you that no factual evidence is presented to support the claims of Putin's meddling in the American presidential election. I don't know whether he did or didn't. But the absence of substantiation doesn't seem to matter to most media outlets.

The Putin-scare created by Clinton worked like a charm to cover over the grim fact that the Democratic Party primaries were illegitimate. That's something that would have made Hillary's own nomination itself illegitimate and undemocratic. It's a very shrewd strategy, and unfortunately many Americans have been tricked by it.

It All Fits Together

The election-scandal story connected so seamlessly with the malicious Trump-Putin tale that one wonders if they weren't both part of a single plan.

This is just speculation, but what if Clinton had

seen signs that the election-rigging story might come out. In preparation, the Clinton people promote the Trump-Putin fear-mongering story. And then when the election scandal breaks, Clinton is ready to cast herself as a victim of the purported Trump-Putin axis of evil. This scenario may sound very diabolical, yet still it is perfectly plausible.

Who is Trump's Putin Connection?

What does the foregoing tell us about who Trump's "Putin connection" is?

It's Hillary.

She's the one that's drawing the connection, and she's doing it out of apparent self-interest and in the absence of facts.

In effect, Hillary has outed herself as Trump's "Putin connection." But few enough people follow this saga in sufficient depth to realize that.

Chapter 3
FORBES FIBBED

Filed: August 1, 2016

Here's a point-by-point refutation of the *Forbes* July 18, 2016 story about Trump's ties to Vladimir Putin referenced in the previous chapter:

The *Forbes* piece was headlined, "Trump, Deferring to Putin, Deleted GOP Platform's Call to Supply Ukraine with Lethal Defensive Weapons."

There isn't anything in this headline that is demonstrably true. Interestingly, that same Trump-Putin theme is being voiced strongly by the Hillary Clinton campaign. Trump is in cahoots with Vladimir Putin they claim. There's been no factual substantiation, though.

Let's pick off a couple of the clearest points.

Fact Check No. 1

Forbes said, "Under Putin, Russia is in the top list of journalists killed for political motives."

The article references the Committee to Protect Journalists as the authority on that. But CPJ's own website puts that story in better perspective. At the time the *Forbes* article was published here is what CPJ's website listed as the 20 deadliest countries for journalists since 1992 (showing how many died in each):

1. Iraq: 174
2. Syria: 96
3. Philippines: 77
4. Algeria: 60
5. Somalia: 59
6. Pakistan: 58
7. Russia: 56
8. Colombia: 47
9. India: 39
10. Brazil: 38
11. Mexico: 36
12. Afghanistan: 29
13. Turkey: 25
14. Bangladesh: 20
15. Sri Lanka: 19

16. Bosnia: 19
17. Rwanda: 17
18. Tajikistan: 17
19. Sierra Leone: 16
20. Israel and the Occupied Palestinian Territory: 16

Although Russia really is in that top 20 list, it clearly does not top the list. That distinction goes to Iraq with 174 deaths. Russia is number 7 with 56 deaths. Philippines is up at number 3. The US Department of state has designated Philippines "a major non-NATO ally." But where's the outcry over that country's very high number of journalist deaths?

Also on the list is NATO ally Turkey, along with US neighbor Mexico plus a number of other US friendly states. Why is *Forbes* singling out Russia?

In contrast to the 2016 CPJ list is its report from 1998, before Putin ever came to power. Back then CPJ ranked Russia as the number 2 deadliest country for journalists. That means Russia's deadliest score slipped from way up at number 2, down to number 7. But *Forbes* makes no mention of that improvement under Putin.

What's the *Forbes'* game here? The CPJ data *Forbes* cited does not really confirm what *Forbes* is alleging.

The magazine is clearly trying to flimflam its
readers. There's something very biased in the
way *Forbes* has singled out Russia for criticism.

(Note: The version of this report published
elsewhere utilized CPJ statistics from an earlier
time. They have been updated above to
correspond with CPJ's current data from the time
frame of the *Forbes* article.)

Fact Check No. 2

Forbes rhetoric suggests these murders in Russia
were political assassinations.

But CPJ instead calls them "Journalists Killed in
Russia/Motive Confirmed." CPJ goes on to
explain:

"We consider a case 'confirmed' only if we are
reasonably certain that a journalist was murdered
in direct reprisal for his or her work; was killed
in crossfire during combat situations; or was
killed while carrying out a dangerous assignment
such as coverage of a street protest."

That covers a lot more territory than the alleged
political assassinations ordered by Putin per the

Forbes article.

It could include a death resulting from a business dispute, a result of a war zone injury, or a result of a domestic protest gone violent, among other things.

Forbes lied. The CPJ statistics are not focused on politically motivated deaths.

Fact Check No. 3

Certainly the 56 journalist deaths in Russia are nothing to brag about. But here's another fact. All those journalist murders for which *Forbes* blames Putin didn't even happen under Putin's watch. Indeed, under Yeltsin there was a higher number of murders per year, 4.3 on average. Under Putin that number dropped to 1.6, almost two-thirds less than Yeltsin's record.

Again *Forbes* misled its readers, plain and simple.

Fact Check No. 3

And just to illustrate the utter vacuousness of the *Forbes* claims: one of the journalists murdered after Putin became president is Paul Klebnikov, an American of Russian decent, and, ironically, then-editor of the Russian edition of *Forbes*.

Klebnikov was no critic of Putin, and indeed actually admired him. According to NBC News, "He saw his ancestral homeland, after years of crime-infused chaos and government corruption, moving forward under a strong leader, President Vladimir Putin."

In these post-Klebnikov days, however, it's become clear that *Forbes* now pursues actively an agenda of provocation and fabrication when it comes to Putin.

Fact Check No. 4

And now to the *Forbes* headline in question: It claims that Trump was "deferring to Putin."

Webster's defines deference as, "respect and esteem due a superior or an elder, or affected or ingratiating regard for another's wishes.

Putin isn't "a superior" or "an elder" to Trump. That means *Forbes* must be suggesting that Trump is carrying out Putin's wishes. But no evidence is presented to support that astonishing claim. Are we just supposed to take *Forbes'* word for it? After its record of outright lies about Putin?

Fact Check No. 5

The *Forbes* article goes on, "According to multiple accounts, the Trump campaign has successfully worked behind the scenes to make sure the new Republican platform would not pledge the lethal defensive weapons Ukraine has been pleading for from the United States."

I don't know whether or not that's true. It is certainly plausible, and indeed, the platform does not contain a pledge to provide lethal defensive weapons to Ukraine.

But in making its case, *Forbes* lies again.

The "multiple accounts" it cites? There are only two given. One is a *Washington Post* article by Josh Rogin. The other is a *New York* magazine article that quotes that same *Washington Post* article by Josh Rogin.

So the "multiple accounts" that upon first glance seem to be only two references, turn out to be just a single source reference, that to the comments of one Josh Rogin.

That's more deception from *Forbes*.

Fact Check No. 6

What did this sole source, Josh Rogin, actually say?

He claims to have inside information from the Republican platform committee. He doesn't explain how he came by that inside information, but apparently just expects us to trust him.

Rogin wrote, "Diana Denman, a platform committee member from Texas who was a Ted Cruz supporter, proposed a platform amendment that would call for maintaining or increasing sanctions against Russia, increasing aid for Ukraine and 'providing lethal defensive weapons' to the Ukrainian military."

So, if we take Rogin at his word, he is saying not that Trump had something deleted from the platform. He's saying that an amendment was proposed but not adopted.

That chalks up another lie for *Forbes*. A platform provision was not deleted as claimed by *Forbes*. Instead, a proposed amendment was simply not accepted as submitted. That puts a different slant on the story.

The Proof's Gone Poof

So now a Trump-Putin nexus has been trumpeted

by many, including *Forbes*, the *New York Times* and others. It has been demonstrated, though, that their attempts to promote a nefarious link between Trump and Putin are based on lies and innuendo.

A Trump-Putin connection? I'm wondering about a *Forbes*-Hillary connection.

Chapter 4
TRUMP FLUBS RESPONSE

Filed: August 2, 2016

Leave it to Trump's campaign to dangerously flub its response to the latest Clinton trap regarding Russia.

Think about this imaginary conversation:

Meet the Press host Chuck Todd to Trump campaign manager Paul J. Manafort:

"What was your role in the Republican platform's call for preemptive bombing North Korea?"

Manafort to Todd: "I had none."

What's the takeaway from this hypothetical exchange?

Manafort validated Todd's assertion that there is a plan for bombing, while claiming to have had no part in it.

But no facts were on the table to show there was any such plan in the first place. Todd asked a trick question, and Manafort fell for it.

That pseudo-conversation illustrates what just happened in real life.

Beyond the Hypothetical

Now the subject is not North Korea, but Ukraine and the recent Clinton allegations that Trump is in cahoots with Vladimir Putin. This is a really big political issue.

Huffington Post ran the headline, "Trump Pushed for GOP to Change Ukraine Position." This supports the Clinton suggestion that Trump is tainted by his alleged connections with Vladimir Putin.

HuffPost went on to say, "The pro-Russia change was the only party platform-tweak the Trump camp cared about, sources say."

By the way, I told *Huffington Post* that I could find no primary source for the issues their story raises, and asked if they have one. There was no immediate response.

The Real Dialogue

Here's the true-life interaction between Manafort and Todd: Sunday morning, July 31, 2016, Manafort appeared with Todd on *Meet the Press*. Todd brought up the platform issue of sending lethal weaponry to Ukraine.

He asked, "How much influence did you have on changing that language?"

Manafort answered, "I had none."

Bingo

That's the same trick from the North Korea hypothetical. It's almost like the old "when did you stop beating your wife?" joke question. Todd set up a false premise and cast an aspersion of Manafort's complicity.

But, instead of denying the legitimacy of the premise, Manafort's first response was to deny his culpability. In doing so, he validated the false premise.

Manafort added, "In fact I didn't even hear about

it until after our convention was over." Again, another validation of the false premise.

What Manafort should have told Todd right off the bat is: "There was no such change in the platform."

An Unwitting Sabotage

The *Meet the Press* exchange is covered in an August 1, 2016 TMZ.com story titled "Changed GOP Platform on Ukraine." While this article piles-on Manafort over Todd's allegations, it also, perhaps unwittingly, sabotage's the Todd-TMZ premise of a platform change.

TMZ.com references a July 18, 2016 *Washington Post* article by Josh Rogin as its source, and summarizes:

"When a platform committee member offered an amendment to the platform that called for supporting Ukraine, members of the Trump campaign who were not members of the committee jumped in to edit the amendment, Rogin reported. They stripped language from the amendment saying the U.S. should help Ukraine by 'providing lethal defensive weapons' and instead wrote that America should offer 'appropriate assistance.'"

Do you see the flaw in the Todd-TMZ argument? An amendment was offered to inject a call for sending lethal weaponry. Trump didn't have the platform changed. It didn't call for lethal weapons in the first place. Someone else tried and failed to make a change.

What's more, it seems like the Trump camp worked to strike up a compromise instead of outright defeating the proposed amendment.

Based on the TMZ.com report it sounds like the amendment would politically mandate sending deadly weapons. The compromise amendment calls for offering "appropriate assistance." Logically if sending lethal weaponry should show itself as appropriate, it would be permissible.

The original proposal was to send the weapons whether they were appropriate or not at any given time. What a dangerous condition that would have created. Thank goodness a compromise was worked out.

Manafort is a sharp, experienced guy. But he's sure blowing it when it comes to the Russia issue.

Actually Manafort is Paul J. Manafort, Jr. He

grew up in the city where I live, where he's known as "PJ." I knew his late father. He was a popular former mayor. We have a street named after him, "Paul Manafort Drive."

I can remember sitting with the senior Manafort one presidential election night years ago in front of a TV. PJ had tipped him off to the time when he would be speaking on a national broadcast network. Paul Sr. was proudly awaiting the appearance of PJ.

PJ's Goof

I think it's sad to see that PJ is unsuccessfully handling the challenges the Clinton campaign are throwing him over Russia. Perhaps Manafort has poor staff support in this area.

Nonetheless we still see the specious Clinton allegations, Todd's successful attempt to put Manafort in a compromised position, and also TMZ's me-too article. Lies, lies, lies, everwhere lies.

The Trump team seems to be the only truthful player here. Yet Trump is getting his clock cleaned over Russia.

This Clinton gamesmanship continues to push

the US-Russia relationship dangerously toward the brink. I think the most effective way to halt that nonsense is to turn the issue back around on Clinton. That should be done. It can be done. But no one's doing it. Alas.

Chapter 5
BUT HILLARY TRIPS UP

Filed: August 3, 2016.

Hillary Clinton tripped herself up while attacking Trump on the DNC leaks.

Amidst the furious Clinton allegations that Donald Trump is in cahoots with Vladimir Putin on the DNC email leaks, Trump made an astonishing statement. He said at a news conference: "Russia, if you're listening, I hope you're able to find the 30,000 emails that are missing; I think you will probably be rewarded mightily by our press."

Well Duh

If you listen to that line in the context of its

surrounding remarks, it's clear that Trump's remark was flippant or sarcastic. Most media outlets, however, pulled it out of context, and the Clinton campaign climbed all over the statement.

Apparently they didn't think their strategy through very well because here's what happened: The media reports asserted that Trump had invited Putin to conduct espionage against the US by hacking national security data. This disqualifies Trump from becoming president, they said. Many called his statement treasonous.

But Here's the Trap

The national security data in question are the 30,000 emails that Clinton deleted from her server, claiming they were just personal chit-chat. But now with apparent witlessness the Clinton camp has upgraded that chit-chat to vital national security information.

The Clinton clan seemed to think it had trapped Trump with his own statement. But in reality, it was Clinton upon whom the jaws of the trap clamped down.

CNBC even did a story and video on this titled "The Democrats just fell for Trump's Russian email-hack bait."

Chapter 6
PUTIN'S ORDERS

So, what are Putin's orders for Trump? The proof is in. Here's what's been documented:

(The following space is deliberately left blank.)

Appendix I
THE AUTHOR

William Dunkerley is a media business analyst and Senior Fellow at American University in Moscow. He has worked on behalf of US interests in promoting press freedom in Eastern Europe and the former Soviet Union. He was commissioned by the International Federation of Journalists to analyze problems in certain Western press coverage of Russian issues. Mr. Dunkerley has been instrumental in shaping laws governing the media in Eastern Europe and Russia and has offered testimony to the United States Congress on media concerns. He has personally done intensive work in seven post communist countries, including interventions in seventeen different cities across all Russia. He is principal of William Dunkerley Publishing Consultants, and publisher of two industry monthlies, *Editors Only* and the *STRAT* newsletter.

Appendix II
THIS SERIES

"Russia: Straight Talk on Hushed Issues" is a monograph series that looks behind the popular headlines and presents iconoclastic analyses. The books explain aspects of mainstream news that are either being distorted, glossed over, or hushed up.

The etiology of these media distortions is complex. Historically there was little harshness in the coverage of Yeltsin's misdeeds, perhaps a result of Western giddiness over the collapse of the Soviet Union.

When Putin entered the scene in 1999 the kid gloves came off. He was demonized. Russian tycoons who had been involved in skullduggery under Yeltsin found the new leader problematic.

Boris Berezovsky, one of the tycoons, carried

media attacks to new heights after fleeing to London in 2001 to evade corruption charges. He packaged and distributed highly engaging news stories with associated graphics and interview opportunities to media outlets worldwide. Probably because of that convenience, they were readily accepted by the media unquestioningly despite their lack of factual bases.

Inexplicably, after Berezovsky's 2014 death, the stream of demonizing stories continued. Had Berezovsky's campaign just made an indelible impression that still taints the views of media and political leaders in the US and elsewhere? Or is there a new kingpin yet to be identified?

Regardless, many people have indeed formed beliefs based on the prevalence of distorted news and are committed to them. It would be unrealistic to think many of these folks will accept any contravening facts and analyses.

So the intention of this series is to give open-minded audiences in the US and other Western countries insights into misleading and fabricated reportage. That should allow them to arrive at more realistic and fact-based understandings, thus facilitating their serving more responsibly as members of our society. The intention is not to exonerate anyone who has been accused, but to point out that the accusers are liars and fabricators. (Note: Monographs in this series appear in no particular order.)

H.G. Wells once said: "Civilization is in a race between education and catastrophe."

But what is now unfolding in the theater of US-Russia relations is a race between catastrophe and utter disaster.

One entrant is the United States, and the other is Russia. Which country is on which side actually makes no difference. In this race, there are allegations, then sanctions, and then retributions for the previous actions. It is a self perpetuating loop.

This is a race in which the winner will personify either political buffoonery or plain stupidity. And which of the two is the victor will also make no difference. The main point for the rest of us is that this race will cause us all to lose.

As part of the "Russia: Straight Talk on Hushed Issues" monograph series, this book is dedicated to ending that foolish race, and to the concept of a safe, sustaining, and positive relationship between the United States and the Russian Federation.

Appendix III
ACKNOWLEDGMENT

In the face of much media misinformation about Russia, I wish to acknowledge the effort and perseverance of all who have spoken and written the honest truth. They have shown great courage in bucking the unfortunate mainstream trend toward fabrication. Their work serves as an essential predicate to this book. --W.D.

www.ingramcontent.com/pod-product-compliance
Lightning Source LLC
Chambersburg PA
CBHW060820260726
48660CB00003B/1017